La

Bethany

....

UNCOVERING THE THEOLOGY BEHIND JESUS RAISING LAZARUS FROM THE DEAD

ORGANIC FAITH SERIES
BOOK THREE

SCOTT DOUGLAS

SD Publications
Anaheim, California
www.JesusAscended.com

Dedicated to Unanswered Prayers

TABLE OF CONTENTS

....

INTRODUCTION

Lazarus is an amazing story. A man rose from the dead! You just don't get any more awesome than that, right?! But is that the only takeaway from the story? Is that what we are supposed to learn from his resurrection? Not exactly.

Jesus performed lots of miracles. John said it best when he said that there would not be room in the whole world to describe all that he did (John 21:25). It's easy to look at the stories of miracles and see them for what they're worth: miracles. But that's a shame. If the miracle is in the Bible, there's a reason for it. It's not just there because it was miraculous.

With Lazarus, a man rose from the dead—an amazing miracle, no doubt. But there's more to it than that.

Lazarus wasn't just a man who raised from the dead—he had a life before and after his resurrection. And Jesus didn't perform the miracle just to be flashy.

There's a story to Lazarus that goes beyond the miracle itself. There's theology to uncover and there's a man that needs to be understood. But most importantly, there's a lesson to be learned.

Scott Douglas

ONE

....

DEAD NO MORE

Resurrection is…miraculous. But unique? I'm going to take a wild guess here and say you've probably never been resurrected. And you probably don't know anyone who has been resurrected. Yes, there are people who claim they've seen the light and been brought back to life. And maybe their stories are true. But they're certainly not everyday occur-rences.

The fact is anytime someone is brought back from the dead it's not like the movies—it's not because they go up to those pearly gates and beg an angel-clad Saint Peter for one more chance. One could even argue that

13

there's a theological reason that they don't even make sense because depending on your views of the afterlife, we don't actually go straight to heaven when we die—we're sort of in a holding pattern until the day that Christ returns.

Views on when we go back to heaven aside, it's fair to say that if a person dies only to come back, there is a reason.

In 2013, after a healthy nine-month pregnancy, my wife and I were hit with news that changed our lives and marriage: the son that she had been carrying for nine months—the one we had named, the one we had bought clothes for, the one who had a Star Wars themed nursery waiting for his arrival—the one we considered a blessing and that we thanked God for—was dead.

Mordecai was due any day. When we went in for a routine test to check his heartbeat, we expected it to be just that: routine. But it was anything but. The heartbeat that had been there just days before was no longer there.

A nurse pulled me aside as they prepared to run more test and told me matter of factly, "You need to prepare yourself for the fact that your son is dead."

Immediately what came to mind was not preparing myself for his death, but Mark 11:23, "If anyone says to this mountain, 'Go, throw yourself into the sea,' and does not doubt in their heart but believes that what they say will happen, it will be done for them."

As I looked at my confused and frightened wife, I prayed over her. I prayed for a miracle. That the mountain would be moved. That our sons heart would beat once more.

We were faithful. We prayed. We went to church. We tithed. We confessed with our lips that Jesus Christ was Lord and believed with our hearts that he was raised from the dead.

We believed.

And the prayer was not answered.

You can interpret that how you want. This book is not on prayer and why God does not always answer them.

But to ask God to give life where it has been taken is no small thing, and history has taught us that when it happens, there is a reason for it.

To help us understand this idea of bringing life to the dead, let's get Biblical. Let's look at places the Bible tells us this quite unusual miracle happened.

The most obvious place to start is with Jesus. He is the most famous case of resurrection for all mankind. Ever.

But Jesus was also a different kind of resurrection.

Where others were resurrected by someone else—by someone telling the person to rise— Jesus rose by his own authority.

But the most striking difference between Jesus and anyone else is what happened after.

Jesus did not die again. Others died only to face death again at another point in their life.

Jesus rose and conquered death. He ascended to heaven.

In the resurrection, Christ defeated sin; in the Ascension, Christ defeated death.

The other cases of resurrection, while miraculous, weren't quite as powerful.

And if you're saying, "Hold on there! I thought you said Jesus was the only person who never died! What about Elijah and Enoch?" I won't get into it here, except to say neither went to heaven on their own doing—something brought them. With Elijah and Enoch, they were "taken up" to heaven—or in the case of Enoch he was taken away...maybe to heaven or maybe just literally taken away somewhere else; Jesus Ascended. The difference is the first two needed help getting there. If you want to get really technical about it, then you can question if Elijah went to heaven at all because, as mentioned earlier, depending on your views of heaven, we don't go there until Christ returns—we essentially wait for him, but we don't know we are waiting...kind of like a really good sleep. But let's not get into that here.

#

Let's get Old Testament for a minute.[1]

When it comes to the dead returning to life, there are three clear examples in the Old Testament (OT) and they all center around the two all-stars of OT prophets: Elijah and Elisha.

If you've never read about the two lively characters, it's high time you do! Elijah was as fiery as they come—he loved to show how powerful God is. And if you think The Miracle Worker was just the name of a movie about Helen Keller, then you obviously haven't read about Elisha. This guy was the original miracle worker—in fact, nobody, except for Moses, performed tmiracles than he.

---

[1] I promise to go easy on you and not sprinkle in verses from Deuteronomy.

In many ways, the two, who for many years worked beside each other,[2] perfectly complemented each other: Elijah was blunt and fearless; Elisha was compassionate and merciful. Many scholars[3] compare these two guys to Qui-Gon Jinn and Obi-Wan Kenobi.

So where are the three miracles that these two guys did? Let's look. The first is 1 Kings 17:17-24 where Elijah prays to God and a young boy comes back from the dead:

Sometime later the son of the woman who owned the house became ill. He grew worse and worse, and finally stopped breathing. She said to Elijah, "What do you have against me, man of God? Did you come to remind me of my sin and kill my son?"

"Give me your son," Elijah replied. He took him from her arms, carried him to the upper

---

[2] Elijah was Elisha's mentor.

[3] You can interpret scholar as I, the author, who is not a scholar.

room where he was staying, and laid him on his bed. Then he cried out to the Lord, "Lord my God, have you brought tragedy even on this widow I am staying with, by causing her son to die?" Then he stretched himself out on the boy three times and cried out to the Lord, "Lord my God, let this boy's life return to him!"

The Lord heard Elijah's cry, and the boy's life returned to him, and he lived. Elijah picked up the child and carried him down from the room into the house. He gave him to his mother and said, "Look, your son is alive!"

Then the woman said to Elijah, "Now I know that you are a man of God and that the word of the Lord from your mouth is the truth." (NIV)

Nice, right? But, like I have said, God doesn't just raise people from the dead for kicks and giggles. There's a reason. So what's going on here? What is the context?

This is actually part of a three-part play of sorts. Scene one is Elijah prophesizing that there will be no rain except by God's word. Scene two, God tells Elijah to live in Zarephath, where God has told a widow, who has no food, to feed him; Elijah gives her oil and proclaims that whatever she gives him will indeed fill him up. And then, finally, scene three, where the miracle happens.

Elijah's chilling with the widow and it seems pretty good; she had no food for her family, and yet God is providing—out of nothing there's still enough to make them feel satisfied. Her son, who probably would have died of starvation, has food. Life is good. And then it is not. Her son is stricken with an illness and dies.

The woman is obviously devastated, and it seems that Elijah is quite shocked as well. I don't think he expected death here either. But he also seems to have more clarity in the situation. He takes a step back and realizes that God wouldn't let all these good things happen only to kill her son. It made no sense to him. And so he says to give him her son. He takes the boy and gets angry with God—he basically says, "What gives! Did you really send me here to watch this kid die?"

You expect Elijah to take a step back at this point; to wait for God to answer. But Elijah's not the waiting type. Instead he stretches himself over the boy three times,[4] then cries to God to let the boy live.

At this point, you are probably expecting the boy to live—but you are also expecting God to reveal why he did it to begin with. That this death carried purpose. Funny thing happens on the way to resurrection: purpose doesn't come. Instead of giving a reason, it just says that God heard Elijah and returned life to the boy. That's it! How anticlimactic, right?!

Here's the thing: bad things happen. And that's life. We can look around and see all the ways God has blessed us—but that doesn't mean our life will not be without suffering.

---

[4] Interpret this as you will, but on the third day, Christ rose from the dead—three in the Bible, if you don't know, usually shows harmony and completeness.

Suffering is a part of life—a part that, for better or worse, helps us appreciate what we have. So in many ways, God has taught this woman a cruel lesson—that just because a blessing has come that doesn't mean all will be peachy. Our faith needs to be strong in both good times and in bad. Our faith needs to be strong enough to withstand the hard times.

This woman's thinking is like most of ours. We have no problem being happy when times are good—see God's beauty and grace in these moments; but then harsh times come and we become angry—we fail to understand that in all things, good and bad, we are being blessed by God.

Not a moment goes by that I don't grieve the loss of my son, but if time has taught me anything, it is that his death was a blessing from God. That doesn't mean I rejoice in it. That doesn't mean I thank God for it. But it does mean I can look at it and understand that while I might not understand the meaning of his death, I understand that God does—that he is the creator and taker of all things and he does all things in love and grace.

And though the woman's thinking is wrong, God has mercy on her when he listens to Elijah. Was Elijah's thinking wrong too? He did get angry at God, after all? You can draw your own conclusions to that, but what we can find harmony in is that Elijah's anger came because he had compassion for the woman. Just as Jesus hurt for the Mary's before he rose Lazarus, Elijah hurt for this woman. He had obviously spent time with her. He knew her situation and the trials she went through. He grieved for her loss and he reacted to it.

So while God does not come down and explain himself, he does show through actions: he shows that he is a compassionate God. In some ways this is a little radical to Hebrew readers of the time—God was known for power…the compassionate side of God is something that we see more of in the New Testament.

The boy lives and God has blessed the woman's life again, but in his death she can learn that suffering will come—that just because God has shown his grace to you and given you good things, doesn't mean life will continue in this way. And when suffering comes, it in no way means that God is no longer blessing you.

The second resurrection comes at the hands of Elisha in 2 Kings 4:32-37. It reads:

> *When Elisha reached the house, there was the boy lying dead on his couch. He went in, shut the door on the two of them and prayed to the Lord. Then he got on the bed and lay on the boy, mouth to mouth, eyes to eyes, hands to hands. As he stretched himself out on him, the boy's body grew warm. Elisha turned away and walked back and forth in the room and then got on the bed and stretched out on him once more. The boy sneezed seven times and opened his eyes.*

Elisha summoned Gehazi and said, "Call the Shunammite." And he did. When she came, he said, "Take your son." She came in, fell at his feet and bowed to the ground. Then she took her son and went out. (NIV)

As has been noted, Elijah was the fiery one, so Elisha's compassion in these verses is not exactly out of the ordinary for him. He gets to the house and where Elijah almost seemed to be yelling at God, Elisha simply gets to the house, sees the dead boy, and goes to the parents to pray with them.

After he prays, he returns to the boy and things get…weird. He doesn't ask God to heal this boy—he instead gets up close and personal with the boy: mouth to mouth, eyes to eyes, hands to hands.

We don't know that much about the woman. We know that she's a believer, but we actually don't know this until hundreds of years later when Hebrews 11:35 recounts this story and tells us that this was a woman of faith. In verse 8, it says the woman was "well-

to-do," (NIV) which some interpret as wealthy
and others interpret as a person of good character—perhaps both. What is accepted is for
richer or poorer, this is a respected woman in
the community.

So she seems to have it all...except for one
thing: a child.

Elisha knows the dilemma—that like a lot
of women, she is faithful and desperately
wants a child, but is barren. But he tells her
not to fret—she's going to have a child.

Just like the other woman, this woman
must have felt truly blessed. God has given
her what she did not have—food for the last
woman, a child for this woman. She has been
rewarded for her faithfulness.

And just like before: the child dies.

It's just as shocking here as the other miracle. Why would God bless a person so abun-
dantly only to allow such tragedy?

So after Elisha prays for the family, he goes
to the boy. And it's a private affair. We see a lot
of flashy preachers today—they love to turn
miracles into spectacles. That's not happening

here—nor should it. Elisha shows that he is just a vessel—he is there as a vessel to restore the boy's relationship with God, which is something that should not be done publicly.

The actions that Elisha's doing in this room certainly look unusual, but metaphorically, there's intimacy here. His closeness with the child—his compassion for him—it warms him…literally. But it's not enough. Then Elisha starts pacing in the room and stretches over him; it's at this action that the boy wakes up and sneezes seven times.[5]

Again, we don't know why God performed the miracle, but we can look at the story and see a teaching—one of faithfulness. Unlike the previous story, there is no doubt or anger— there is only faithfulness. At no time did anyone question God. And for their faithfulness they were rewarded.

And now we come to the last story. Elisha is "technically" responsible for this one as well

---

[5] In the Bible, seven usually shows completeness— God is done with something. God created the world in seven days, for example.

—but it's not what you think. You'll find the encounter in 2 Kings 13:21:

Once while some Israelites were burying a man, suddenly they saw a band of raiders; so they threw the man's body into Elisha's tomb. When the body touched Elisha's bones, the man came to life and stood up on his feet. (NIV)

So this guy is healed because he touched Elisha's bones.[6] Who said miracles couldn't be gross? But fans of the New Testament will hopefully also see the obvious parallel in this story with the person who touches Jesus and is healed.[7]

There's a lot of symbolism in this story. You might even say it's more of a reminder than a lesson: a reminder that even though Elisha is dead, God has not forgotten him.

---

[6] You can interpret bones there as Elisha was a little...rotten.

[7] Matthew 9:20-22 and Matthew 14:36.

This is the third miracle—and remember three means harmony and completeness? Fitting that this is the last type of resurrection miracle in the Old Testament, isn't it?

The story tells of a man who has died and they're on their way to bury him—but then they learn there are raiders on their tail,[8] and so they ditch the body in Elisha's tomb. The man's body rolls inside until it hits Elisha's corpse, then bam! He's up walking around again!

One can imagine this guy goes on to be a living testimony of God—that they didn't need to worry about those raiders because God is with them—even though the great prophet is gone, God remains with them.

#

See! I promised no weird laws from the Old Testament. And now we can return to our regularly scheduled broadcast in the New Tes-

---

[8] Probably Moabites.

tament. In the Gospels, there are four accounts of resurrection of life—three that Christ did, and then, of course, the resurrection of Christ, which was technically also performed by Christ.

Starting with Luke, there is the raising of Widow of Nain's son. It reads:

Soon afterward, Jesus went to a town called Nain, and his disciples and a large crowd went along with him. As he approached the town gate, a dead person was being carried out—the only son of his mother, and she was a widow. And a large crowd from the town was with her. When the Lord saw her, his heart went out to her and he said, "Don't cry."

Then he went up and touched the bier they were carrying him on, and the bearers stood still. He said, "Young man, I say to you, get up!" The dead man sat up and began to talk, and Jesus gave him back to his mother.

They were all filled with awe and praised God. "A great prophet has appeared among us," they said. "God has come to help his people." This news about Jesus spread throughout Judea and the surrounding country. (NIV)

To understand this story, we have to look to the Old Testament. I know, I know! I promised we were done. But we have to go back to go forward. In Isaiah 35:4-6, we get the following Messiac prophecy:

"Be strong, do not fear; your God will come, he will come with vengeance; with divine retribution he will come to save you."

Then will the eyes of the blind be opened and the ears of the deaf unstopped.

Then will the lame leap like a deer, and the mute tongue shout for joy. Water will gush forth in the wilderness and streams in the desert. (NIV)

Now let's go back to Luke and thumb forward just a few verses to verse 22. John the Baptist's followers ask Jesus if he's the Messiah they've been waiting for and he replies in Luke 7:22:

So he replied to the messengers, "Go back and report to John what you have seen and heard: The blind receive sight, the lame walk, those who have leprosy are cleansed, the deaf hear, the dead are raised, and the good news is proclaimed to the poor. (NIV)

Instead of telling them that he is the Messiah, he proves it by showing the prophecy he has fulfilled; but he's done more than fulfilled it—he's added to it—not only are people being healed, but people are coming back to life!

As we look at this story, we should be careful to see that this is not just the son of a widow. This is her *only* son. So what Luke is doing is making sure the reader knows how dire the situation is for this woman. The son is supposed to take care of the widow. If one dies and there are no other sons, then her very means of survival is taken from her. It was hard enough that her son died, but it's even harder when you consider that she had literally no one left to make sure she was taken care of. To put it more Biblically, Jesus' "heart went out to her"—he had compassion for her.

The people are in awe at the healing. "Awe" is a common theme to the Luke miracle stories. We frequently see him using words like in "awe" and "astonished" to describe the crowd's response. Then they say, "A great prophet has appeared among us." This emphasis on Jesus being a prophet is also an important theme in Luke; Luke makes several references to Jesus being a Messiac prophet.

Perhaps the most important detail here and in most of the stories is how Jesus helped the widow; when we look at miracles, it's common for Jesus to be helping someone who could not help themself. The miracles show that a new covenant has rolled into town and it is about God coming not for one people, but for all people.

The next resurrection miracle is found in Matthew (Matthew 9:18-26), Mark (Mark 5:21–43), and Luke (Luke 8:40-56). The triple whammy tells the reader that this is a big one. The miracle involves the daughter of Jarius. Let's look at just one of the stories, Matthew 9:18-26:

While he was saying this, a synagogue leader came and knelt before him and said, "My daughter has just died. But come and put your hand on her, and she will live." Jesus got up and went with him, and so did his disciples.

Just then a woman who had been subject to bleeding for twelve years came up behind him and touched the edge of his cloak. She said to herself, "If I only touch his cloak, I will be healed."

Jesus turned and saw her. "Take heart, daughter," he said, "your faith has healed you." And the woman was healed at that moment.

When Jesus entered the synagogue leader's house and saw the noisy crowd and people playing pipes, he said, "Go away. The girl is not dead but asleep." But they laughed at him. After the crowd had been put outside, he went in and took the girl by the hand, and she got up. News of this spread through all that region. (NIV)

The literary device being used here is called intercalation. What's that? It's when one story is inserted into another and linking them together—i this case the connection is between the person with the 12-year ailment and the girl being 12.

Basically what is going on here is the delay in the person being healed for 12 years strengthened their faith. I don't like to use the phrase all things happen for a reason, but I do like to say nothing that happens cannot be used to make your faith stronger. And that's what has happened here.

The beauty in both of these stories is Jesus in each reaches out to the unclean. The woman was impure because of her condition and would have been considered untouchable; and the child was dead—touching corpses was a major no-no for Jewish people. Touching the woman and girl meant that Jesus was also making himself unclean.

And finally we have the story of Lazarus and the Resurrection of Christ, which I won't cover in this chapter.

Scattered throughout the New Testament are more stories of the dead being raised. And it was not only Jesus doing them. Throughout his ministry, Jesus had called the Apostles to go forth and, amongst other things, give life to the dead. You could read that as spiritually dead, of course, but I think it's fair to say many of these healings were far more than spiritual.

And according to the Gospel of Matthew, after Jesus rose, there were dead people all over coming out of their tombs and entering the city.[9]

Outside of the Gospel, we also read about life being given back to the dead in the other books. Paul, for instance, ever the talker, is giving an all-nighter sermon in Acts 20:7-12; Eutychus, one of Paul's traveling buddies, does his best to hang in there—but then he quite literally can't hang in there…he falls asleep sitting on a window sill, falls back-yards, and dies.[10] Paul realizes maybe the middle of the night isn't the best time for a long sermon, so he takes pity on Eutychus and raises him from the dead.

Some have said that Eutychus was never *really* dead. This book isn't to argue that, so I'll leave it at that. However you interpret it, it is clear that Eutychus was healed. You don't fall

---

[9] It was basically the Christian equivalent of the *Night of the Living Dead*—to us it sounds miracu-lous, but to those in the city, it was probably quite terrifying.

[10] Anyone else feel like this verse is better suited for Life of Brian than the book of Acts?

from a three-story window and get up like nothing happened. And yet that is exactly what Eutychus did after Paul healed him.

These type of healings continued outside of the Bible. There are lots of stories about early Christian leaders raising the dead. So just like today, it may not have been the most typical miracle, but it did happen.

Scott Douglas

TWO

....

LAZARUS, A FRIEND OF JESUS

LAZARUS: A BIOGRAPHY

-

So now that we know about all the other accounts of dead coming back to life, let's look at this book's namesake: Lazarus of Bethany.

Are you ready for his epic bio? To learn all about who this guy was that Jesus found to be worthy of bringing back from the dead and teaching this important lesson? Strap yourself in…

Lazarus was…a friend of Jesus.

That's a little anti-climatic, right? You kind of expect Lazarus to be someone great…or heck, you'd expect him to be just someone! Anyone! But the fact is, we really don't know much about who he was—we do, however, know a little about who he became.[11]

The full bio of Lazarus is found in John 11:1-3:

Now a man named Lazarus was sick. He was from Bethany, the village of Mary and her sister Martha. (This Mary, whose brother Lazarus now lay sick, was the same one who poured perfume on the Lord and wiped his feet with her hair.) So the sisters sent word to Jesus, "Lord, the one you love is sick." (NIV)

So from that short little snippet, we know that Lazarus was from Bethany and his sisters

---

[11] More on that soon.

were the famous Mary and Martha duo; Mary famously poured expensive perfume on Jesus' feet and wiped it with her hair.[12] Finally, we know that he was one Jesus loved.

Jesus obviously loves everyone. He loves you. He loves me. He even loves that guy who seems like he hates everyone. But the way it is phrased here, "the one you love," implies that this is a very good friend of Jesus.

We also know his name, obviously, Lazarus. His name comes from Hebrew[13] and means "God has helped." That tells us that he was probably Jewish.

So we don't know if Lazarus was married. We don't know what he did for a living. We don't know how old he was. We don't even know what he looked like. But we do know that Mary and Martha lived with him, which meant they were either single or widowed. That's really it.

---

[12] See Matthew 26, Mark 14, or John 12.

[13] Eleazar.

A TALE OF TWO MEN

Imagine having a name like Samuel Jackson. It's a cool name. Until you get asked for the hundredth time if you are *that* Samuel Jackson, or until you go on a job interview and they do a background check, and they see there are several people with that name in prison, and more than a few show up on a list of sex offenders.

Unfortunately, this case of mistaken identity is something many Biblical figures experienced. So let's take a quick detour to make sure one thing is understood. Lazarus wasn't a beggar.

Well, he could have been a beggar—like I said, we know little about him—but he wasn't the beggar in Luke 16:19-31, who was also named Lazarus.

Some early Christians did mistake the two. Just like today, early Christians had this not-so-great habit of saying things without actually checking them out. And so it did spread in the church that the two were one in the same.

There's even early Christian artwork that depicts Lazarus as a beggar.

LAZARUS AFTER HE WAS RAISED FROM THE DEAD

So we don't know much about before Jesus came to Lazarus and rose him. We do know what happened when he did raise him. But what about the next day and all the days that followed? Lazarus did, after all, die again, right?

You have to image that if you got a second shot like he did, you would be living a pretty different life. You don't come back from the dead and then act like nothing happened. You are a changed person.

So what of Lazarus? Do we know anything? Kind of. But a lot is based on traditions, and traditions have a way of being sort of true and sort of not.

Lazarus does make a second appearance in the Bible. Six days after he rose,[14] John 12:1-3 tells us that it was Lazarus' home that Jesus went to for dinner. This is where Mary pours the expense perfume on Jesus' feet.

Later in the chapter,[15] it says that the chief priests, in addition to wanting to kill Jesus, were also plotting to kill Lazarus because many Jews believed in Jesus because of him.

So this is where Lazarus' story ends. Did the chief priests get their way? Probably not. If they had, it would have most definitely been documented by at least one Gospel writer or mentioned somewhere.

The fact that Jews were believing in Jesus because of Lazarus, however, is telling; it helps makes the case that Lazarus wasn't just sort of in a coma, but not really dead; these people knew just how dead he was because it

---

[14] And hopefully after a nice long shower to get rid of the rotting corpse smell.

[15] John 12:9-11.

was enough to make them believe after hearing about him being raised.

And what about tradition? It can't be entirely trusted, but are there nuggets of truth we can dig out?

There are essentially two traditions. One from Eastern Orthodoxy's and one from Roman Catholics.

If you ask someone in the Eastern Orthodox Church, "Hey, what happened with that Lazarus guy?" it's going to sound a little something like this: Lazarus was a man on the run. As noted in the Bible, there were people who wanted him dead. So after the Resurrection of Christ, Lazarus[16] hightailed it out of Judea and made his way to Cyprus. Cyprus is an island in the Mediterranean Sea just south of Turkey and north of Israel.

In Cyprus, Lazarus allegedly met up with Paul and Barnabas, who eventually appointed him as the first bishop of the Cyprus city of

---

[16] Or Lasso, as nobody called him.

Kition.[17] He led the church there many years, then died about 30 years later, and this time did not come back from the dead.

Is it true? In 890, a tomb was found in Larnaca that bared his name. It read "Lazarus the friend of Christ." You can still visit the tomb today. Does that mean it's legit? Not really. Early Christians had a messy habit of hearing a legend, then helping that legend out a little by scribbling some notes that made the case for it.

The case for a Lazarus heated up even more in 1972 when human remains we found under the alter of the church. Was it Lazarus? Who knows.

Fantastic! So there's some maybe true, maybe not so true stuff there, but good old Lasso did find his place in church history. Correct...but then there's that other tradition.

---

[17] Today it is called Larnaka.

According to Catholics,[18] Lazarus made his way with his sisters Mary and Martha to Provence, which was in the South of France. From there the three parted ways because they wanted to preach the gospel to as many people as possible. So Lazarus went to Marseille[19] where he ultimately became Bishop.

This tradition holds a more violent future of Lazarus. As early Christians were being persecuted, Lazarus was rounded up, imprisoned, and finally beheaded. His body was then buried in Autumn Cathedral.

These two legends aside, there are actually a few alleged tombs of Lazarus. During the Middle Ages, there was big money to be made off pilgrims traveling to see Christian relics, so it's no surprise that people found ways to profit off him.

Great! So which one is true?

---

[18] And by Catholics, I don't mean all Catholics because this is more of a medieval tradition than fact.

[19] Also in the South of France.

Both traditional accounts have Lazarus fleeing, which seems to hold true with what the Bible implied. If chief priests wanted him dead before Jesus resurrected, you better believe they wanted him gone after.

The Bible's reference to many Jews becoming Christians because of him certainly put a target on his head. The disciples were no doubt a thorn in the Jewish leaders' sides, but they probably felt they weren't really doing harm—it was all Jesus. But Lazarus—he was in fact doing harm; his story was converting people, and they wanted to crush it.

But what about after he fled? Did he go to Cyprus or France? We know that Cyprus was visited by early Christians and the gospel spread very early there. In France, however, there are not as many records; the first written record of a Christian in France is actually from the second century. Were they there before that? Yes. But were they there shortly after Jesus' resurrection? And further was Lazarus a Bishop there? It's definitely a harder case to be made, but not impossible.

Perhaps a better question than which is true, however, is why is it so important to you? The importance of Lazarus, at least for theology, is in why the miracle happened, not who Lazarus became.

THE LAZARUS TOMB TODAY

The tomb that Lazarus was resurrected from has a history not quite as complicated. Not quite as complicated, that is, in that there is only one. Complicated in the sense, however, that it may or may not be where the tomb actually was.

It's complicated because after the Bible account, there's relative silence for hundreds of years. Then in the fourth century the site pops up again in the writings of Eusebius of Caesarea.

So it wasn't like someone thought to put orange cones around the site with a big billboard that said, "Lazarus rose from the dead here."

Archeologists do believe that the area which has been declared the site was indeed a cemetery, and it was in the general vicinity of where Lazarus lived. But is this really the tomb? Possibly. Possibly not.

Realistically, it probably is not the tomb. Remember that Lazarus was basically run out of town after the miracle, so it's unlikely that people would be able to keep the site up because Jewish leaders would have condemned the practice.

It makes more sense that 300 some odd years later, when being a Christian was not quite as difficult, that Christians would have begun saying, "Hey! We should take a pilgrimage to this place that the Bible talks about." So then they had to find the now forgotten site. They found the town. They found *a* tomb. It was a nice tomb, so why not slap Lazarus' name on it and make some tourist money from it?

The site became so important that Catholics, Greek Orthodox, and even Muslims built a church to commemorate the site.

Why did Muslims want to build a church there? Lazarus is not mentioned in the Quran after all. While Lazarus is not in the Quran, he does become an important person is Islamic medieval folklore. The Quran also mentions Jesus raising the dead, so it is an important teaching to the religion.

Scott Douglas

THREE

....

THERE'S SOMETHING ABOUT JOHN

When it comes to Lazarus, we know about Mary and Martha from Luke, and we know Jesus was in Bethany from Matthew, but it's the Gospel of John that gets all the glory when it comes to bringing Lazarus back from the dead.

I know we're all eager to get to the actual story, but we need to get all Kelly Clarkson for a moment and *Breakaway* one more time before we unpack the full Lazarus account.

We need to do this because there's something about the John narrative, and it's important.

John was a philosopher and writing to the Greeks. Of all the Gospel prose, his was the most poetic. There are lots of literary devices being used. The entire opening of John, "In the beginning was the Word, and the Word was with God, and the Word was God" (NIV)[20] follows a literary pattern that is also used in the Genesis creation account. John is using it to show that God is creating life all over again—a new creation comes with Christ.

John employs Genesis again with Jesus' final words, "It is finished,"[21] which echoes what God says when creation is finished, "Completed."[22]

---

[20] John 1:1.

[21] John 19:30.

[22] Genesis 2:1.

That's all pretty, but what's it have to do with Lazarus? The first part of John[23] is known as the "Book of Signs." Unlike other Gospels where miracles and teachings occur in a more chronological way, John structures the Gospel differently. There are four parts: the Prologue,[24] the Book of Signs, the Book of Glory,[25] and the Epilogue.[26]

There's some debate about what should be included as miracles in John, but it's almost unanimously accepted that there are at least seven:

1. Changing water into wine.[27]
2. The healing of the royal official's son.[28]

---

[23] It starts at John 1:19 and ends at John 12.

[24] John 1:1-18.

[25] John 13:1 to 20:31.

[26] John 21.

[27] John 2:1-11.

[28] John 4:46-54.

3. The healing of the paralytic.[29]
4. Feeding 5,000.[30]
5. Jesus walking on water.[31]
6. The healing of the blind man.[32]
7. The raising of Lazarus.[33]

When you put all of these miracles or signs together, you have what's known as New Creation Theology.

Kind of has a new-age-y sound to it, doesn't it? Don't break out the Peyote and start questioning how to have a Lotus rebirth because the concept has been around for a while. New Creation Theology is the idea of people having new life and new creation—in other words being reborn.

---

[29] John 5:1-15.

[30] John 6:5-14.

[31] John 6:16-24.

[32] John 9:1-7.

[33] John 11:1-45.

All of the miracles have different meanings, but you can look at each of them and see they have a common theme: new life is given to old life. The concept is pretty glaring in five of the seven, but you may be wondering: how does feeding 5,000 people or walking on water play into that? True, they're pretty impressive miracles, but new creation?

The feeding of the 5,000 was all about the substance we needed to have this new creation—it's God breathing life into us. And Jesus on water was essentially Christ showing his disciples that he *was* the new creation.

In many ways, however, the signs of John are meant to show us the path of believers. With water into wine we witness how before we can really begin our journey, God must cleanse our soul. Next Jesus heals the officials son, and we can see how once we are cleansed, we are able to witness the authority of God. The next sign is important, but we should also consider when the signs take place: the Sabbath. This kind of thing was a major no-no for Jews—you couldn't work on the Sabbath! Even if it was to help someone!

Each of these miracles help us see the shift in the new creation that God is giving us. The rules that we used to be bound by are no more. With new creation we have a new path of discipleship.

Curiously the fourth miracle—the middle miracle in this group of seven—is a bridge between old and new; there are parallels here taken from crossing the Red Sea in the Old Testament.

Then Jesus walks on water—which you might also say parallels the crossing of the Red Sea, only here he walks on top of water versus through it (with God's help). Next we have another miracle performed on the Sabbath.

And finally, we come to Lazarus, which happened to be the last straw in terms of miracles—once he performed this miracle, Jesus was a marked man. But ultimately it's the final step of this New Creation Theology—we are cleansed, our heart is prepared, we have accepted the authority of Christ: we are ready to be reborn.

This idea of new life and new creation is all over John—he's aiming to help show these Greek thinkers what it means to have new life.

So as we go forward and consider the theology and teachings found in Lazarus' miraculous healing, we should also remember that it's part of a larger section of John that is trying to show the concept of new creation.

Scott Douglas

FOUR

....

UNRAVELLING LAZARUS

So we know a little more about Lazarus and who he became. And we know a little more about the context John was writing in. But what of the actual miracle. Is it just that? A miracle? Hardly.

John and all of the Gospel writers were careful with the miracles. They didn't just add them for giggles. John points out that Jesus did more than he could ever fit in all the books of the world. It's clear that Jesus didn't just do the miracles recorded in the Bible. He did many, many more.

And so when we read any miracle in the gospel, it's important to stop and ask why. Why are they in the Bible? Why this miracle and not another? It wasn't because the other miracles were somehow weaker. Every miracle is a teaching. So always ask when you read them what is being taught.

Let's dig into the story in John 11:1-44 and try and make sense of what is going on.

The story opens with Jesus learning that Lazarus is sick. Jesus responds by saying it's not going to end in death. Jesus and Lazarus are close, so if he was *really* sick, then he would have gone immediately to them—or that's what the disciples assumed anyway.

It doesn't say what Lazarus was sick with, but it seems clear that whatever it was, it wasn't the kind of thing you die from. In John 11:11-13 it says:

*After he had said this, he went on to tell them,
"Our friend Lazarus has fallen asleep; but I am
going there to wake him up."*

*His disciples replied, "Lord, if he sleeps, he will
get better." Jesus had been speaking of his
death, but his disciples thought he meant natural sleep. (NIV)*

The fact that the disciples don't understand
what Jesus is saying tells us that they aren't
concerned about Lazarus—they figure he's
just sleeping off whatever he is fighting, but
he's obviously going to get better.

Sleep seems like an odd choice of words to
describe someone who's...you know—dead.
But Jesus is actually choosing the phrase that
was commonly used in the Old Testament.
Think about all those stories of Kings in the
Old Testament. It frequently would not say
that they died, but rather slept.

A little earlier in the chapter, John also puts
a special emphasis on the "light" motif. John
11:9-10 says:

Jesus answered, "Are there not twelve hours of daylight? Anyone who walks in the daytime will not stumble, for they see by this world's light. It is when a person walks at night that they stumble, for they have no light." (NIV)

This light motif is popular with John. Light is all over John. We need to walk in the light. Anyone who hates his brother is in darkness. Whoever loves is in the light. When Jesus heals the blind man in John 9, he doesn't tell him that he's going to give him sight; rather, he tells him that he is the light of the world. He's giving him light—and that's what heals him.

The miracle in this story isn't the dead receiving life. It's the receiving light. That's what we need to look to. That's what Jesus wants us to see here: to find the light. But the light here isn't just for Lazarus—it's for all of us.

Jesus is telling the disciples that they will not stumble when they have faith. That's what this entire miracle is about. It's about having the light of Christ—the resurrection of Lazarus from the dead should be more of a footnote. Jesus is trying to teach us here what it means to trust in him. It's not about receiving a miracle. It's about receiving the light.

Jesus didn't have to come to Lazarus at all. He could have healed from afar. In fact, that would have been the preferred method of healing here because coming into the city would have been dangerous for him. Jewish leaders were watching out for him—looking for any reason to arrest him. He knew full well what coming to Lazarus meant. But he still went. It shows both how much he loved Lazarus and how much he loves us—there is no danger that will stop God from coming.

If there's no danger that will stop God from coming to our rescue, then it is fair to talk about the elephant in the room: why did Jesus wait before coming to Lazarus?

In verse 6, it says Jesus decided not to go right away. He stayed for two days. He knew what was going to happen, but he stayed for two days.

Why didn't he come sooner? He could have spared poor ol' Lazzy a shower.

Did Jesus let Lazarus die—let his poor family suffer and mourn—just to prove a point?

Not exactly.

We know that Lazarus has been dead for four days when Jesus gets there, so he was actually already dead when he was told he was just sick. Let's look at the timeline of events.

Day 1 - Messengers depart to tell Jesus that Lazarus is sick. It's a 20-mile walk, which is about a day's journey. Most likely, Lazarus dies shortly after they leave.

Day 2 - Jesus gets the news. So, again, at this point Lazarus is probably already dead and they just don't know it yet.

Day 3 and 4 - Jesus spends two days in Bethabara.

Day 5 - Jesus leaves Bethabara for Bethany and raises Lazarus.

Jesus knew that Lazarus was dead before he even left for Bethany. How does he know and when? The Bible doesn't say, but you get the feeling that he probably knew even as the messengers came to him and told him that he was sick. But it also tells something about the nature of God: just because God is informed of our troubles doesn't mean he is going to immediately act on them; he acts at the right time and not a minute sooner.

Wouldn't immediately after Lazarus dies be as good as time as any to raise him from the dead? Why four days?

There's more you need to understand: Jewish custom. According to custom, when a person died, their soul would stick around for three days then depart their body. So Jesus actually arrives when Lazarus is soul dead according to Jewish custom.

What difference does it make? Soul or not the guy was still raised from the dead, right? Still a miracle, right? Depends on who you ask. Technically if it's been three days, then he's not really dead. Jews could make the case that his soul had just returned. But at four days the decaying starts and the person is dead both figuratively and spiritually. That kind of miracle shows authority—it shows you are above death.

So four days have passed and sweet little Lazzy is dead-dead. It's time for Jesus to come into town and shake things up.

And shake up is exactly what's going to happen if Jesus comes into this town. As I said earlier, it's not the safest place for him to be. To make matters worse, he doesn't have the best support system. Peter and John aren't exactly giving him encouraging words. But someone else is—a person who could easily be called one of the unlikely heroes of this chapter: Thomas.

I've always felt a bit bad for Thomas. He went down in history as the doubter. Doubting Thomas. But in verse 16, there's a side of Thomas we don't always consider. It says:

Then Thomas (also known as Didymus[a]) said to the rest of the disciples, "Let us also go, that we may die with him." (NIV)

We don't see Doubting Thomas here. We see Loyal Thomas.

In verse 21, Jesus makes his grand entrance to Lazarus' town and is greeted by Martha, who basically tells Jesus that he is too late. There are many teachings in this story, but one of the first ones is here: God is never late.

Sometimes man's clock and God's clock operate on two different schedules. The fact that we don't see our prayers answered when we want them to be answered is not the absence of God's grace, rather the absence of our patience.

Frequently, we are in a trial and then it's over and we feel defeated. We feel like we asked for something. God didn't come through. And we stop asking. The lesson here is never stop asking. Never stop praying. Never give up. Not until you see the miracle— whatever it is.

You want your loved one to be healed. They are not. They die instead. Never stop praying! Never stop talking to God. Is God going to raise them from the dead? Probably not. You don't have to pray for that. Pray for a blessing. In suffering, God comes through: God's grace is revealed. Pray for that revelation.

Where Martha may lack a little patience, she does give a strong example of how we should react to tragedy. She's not angry with God. She even says she still believes that Jesus can do anything. In grief, Martha remains strong.

That's not to say if we curse God in our moment of grief that we will get bad things; God understands our pain and he's forgiving of it. But it is to say that this verse really shows the character of Martha and how strong her faith is.

Next, Martha starts talking about the resurrection of life. It's cue in for Jesus to snap his fingers and say, "I'm going to resurrect that brother of yours." But he doesn't. In verse 25 he says:

> *I am the resurrection and the life. The one who believes in me will live, even though they die;*
> *(NIV)*

It's a powerful thing. Instead of saying "I will give you resurrection" he says, "I am the resurrection." Jesus is showing ultimate authority. He has the power to do all things.

One thing that may be missed in this powerfully moving conversation between Jesus and Martha is where it's taking place. In verse 30, we see that Jesus has not yet entered the village, which is important; it's important because all of this has been happening in relatively private settings. Jesus doesn't want to go and grieve with everyone. He's offering intimacy to the sisters.

Obviously the raising of the dead is what got people excited, but the number two thing people talk about here is the powerfully short verse: "Jesus wept."[34] Much has been written about this verse, which is the shortest verse in the entire Bible. I've always been amazed that this is one of the most powerful verses in the Bible and it only takes two words to reveal God's grace. God doesn't need an epic speech to tell us how things are. He doesn't need a book. He doesn't need chapters. He only needs two words: Jesus wept. In that short verse, so much about God is revealed.

Some might have expected Jesus to lecture Mary and Martha. To tell them, "Why are you weeping? You know that there is an afterlife. You know that you will see your brother

---

[34] John 11:35.

again. You know all of this and you still weep?" For a believer in Christ, dead should be the end of the race—our reward is upon us. So they should be joyful, right? Jesus should remind them of that, no? But he doesn't. He cries with them.

Before we talk more about this verse, let's talk a little more about death. Death isn't a good thing. We shouldn't rejoice in it. It's not natural. It wasn't in God's ultimate plan.

To understand that, you need to go to Genesis. The story of Adam and Eve. Look at Genesis 3:22:

And the Lord God said, "The man has now become like one of us, knowing good and evil. He must not be allowed to reach out his hand and take also from the tree of life and eat, and live forever." (NIV)

What that verse is telling us is that if Adam and Eve had not sinned, they would have been able to continue to eat from that tree—

they would have been alive today. They would have had eternal life on Earth.

Death is not good in Jesus' eyes—death is the enemy. God had not intended for us to experience it. He knew the pain it would bring. Jesus knows that pain here, and he weeps.

Jesus knows what's going to happen. He knows that Lazarus will be raised. So he's not weeping that Lazarus has experienced death. He's weeping for the pain of those around him—that they are experiencing sorrow. Jesus is showing the sympathy that he has for man —that he understands and has compassion. He doesn't just know our pain: he experiences our pain.

Christ obviously has two sides: the human side and the God side. The human side of Christ is on full display here. He's showing a very real human emotion. He's showing that he goes through the same emotions that we go through.

###

Once Jesus weeps, the big moment comes. They walk out to the tomb and Jesus says to move away the stone at the tomb. Martha doesn't want to move it because she says it would stink.[35] This is a gruesome image, but an important one. It needs to be clear to future readers and believers that Lazarus wasn't just in a coma—that Jesus didn't actually raise him from the dead. He is dead—a rotting, stinking corpse—he's going to look and smell like the things that nightmares are made of if they roll that stone away.

But we should also understand here that Jesus isn't just bringing a dead man to life— the soul of Lazarus has left him. What's in that tomb is a corpse. That's it. So there's a double miracle here—as I mentioned earlier, it's been four days, so according to Jewish custom, not only that Jesus brought him back to life, but that he returned the soul back to his body.

Things in the Bible don't often happen as you'd expect, which is clear with what hap-

---

[35] John 11:39.

Scott Douglas

pens next. Jesus looks up to the heavens and you expect him to make his request: to ask God to raise Lazarus. He doesn't. In John 11:41-42 he says:

> *"Father, I thank you that you have heard me. I knew that you always hear me, but I said this for the benefit of the people standing here, that they may believe that you sent me." (NIV)*

Jesus doesn't have to ask God. God knows his heart—he and the father are one. So instead he simply thanks God. But it also implies that Jesus had talked it out with God earlier—they had a conversation. It shows the closeness that Jesus had to God—his ability to talk to him—which illustrates the guide of prayer we can also have. We don't know what happened in the two days that Jesus waited, but considering the fact that God and Jesus have already chatted, then it's possible that this happened during the two days.

In verse 42, Jesus gives a pretty clear reason for why this miracle has happened when he explains to God:

I knew that you always hear me, but I said this for the benefit of the people standing here, that they may believe that you sent me." (NIV)

This miracle was not so people could be in awe—that they could see what this great dude Jesus could do. It was to help them believe not in Jesus the miracle worker, but Jesus the Messiah.

Finally, in verse 43, Jesus performs the miracle by saying, "Lazarus, come out!" Jesus performs miracles in many different ways,[36] and much has been said about what he does here. Many have speculated that if he had not said Lazarus' name that every dead man around would have come out.

I don't think that's the case. I think Jesus had complete control over who he healed and

---

[36] Like spitting in a man's eyes.

why. I think it all goes back to Jesus showing that this was a friend—that he knew him personally—he knew his name.

Then in verse 44, Jesus tells Lazarus to take off his grave clothes and "let him go" (NIV); what's that last part all about? Christ is saying to let go of sin: death has been defeated.

Death is not a good thing. But Jesus ultimately shows that he can defeat death. In Christ, we no longer have to experience this pain called death. Christ has defeated death.

There's both beauty and irony in what happens after this miracle. Beginning in John 11:45 we hear of the plot to kill Jesus. It's the action of giving life that sets in motion the action of taking Jesus' own life.

But how beautiful is this? It's foreshadowing what Jesus' death ultimately would represent: that he dies so we can live.

We don't often think about Grace when we consider the raising of Lazarus, but we should. Jesus had to have known that raising Lazarus from the dead would cost him his own life. If he had simply listened to his disciples and not gone to this dangerous city—perhaps just did the miracle from afar—then he could have gone to a village a little more... friendly. He could have continued teaching in places that would welcome him.

But he didn't.

He went to see Lazarus and gave his finest teaching: that he would give his life, so someone else could live.

Before we end, it's important to talk about the concept of sleep. I'm not talking about the kind you do at night—although, let's be honest, you need more of that...your mother's worried about you.

The sleep I'm talking about is the one I mentioned earlier—the dead kind of sleep. Why is Jesus talking about Lazarus sleeping here? And why is sleep so commonly used in the Old Testament to describe death?

We've all heard the stories about people returning from the dead—if not personally, we've surely seen them on Oprah. They talk about the light. About seeing Jesus or some other Biblical figure like Peter. About pearly gates.

Are they true or is there some other explanation? I don't know.

Here's what I do know: Lazarus was clinically dead for four days. Most people who die and see something are clinically dead for a few minutes, then are resuscitated and brought back to life. In that short time they have a book's worth of material about what they saw on the other side.

Lazarus had all these people beat. He wasn't gone for a few minutes...or even hours. He was gone for a few days! What did he bring back with him? Here's the thing: we don't know.

Kind of unusual isn't it? That's not to say he didn't see anything. Maybe he saw something and it's not recorded; but if that's the case, why? Why wouldn't you want to record it? It had to be some crazy experience! He had to have seen a lot!

Unless he didn't see anything at all.

It really begs the question: what happened to Lazarus when he died. And the answer to that, as is the answer to many things in the Bible: It's complicated.

It really depends on your view of the afterlife. And that's where this whole notion of "sleep" comes into play.

Many people prefer to have a rosy view of heaven. That once we die we float on up to the great beyond. Sorry to break it to you, but that's the Hollywood version of heaven.

Here's the truth about death that we don't always hear in Sunday school: we don't go to heaven when we die. When Jesus talks about Lazarus "sleeping" it's because that's the actual Biblical definition of death; the Bible says when we die we are basically in a state of sleeping where we don't know anything—we don't remember it—it's an unconscious state.

It's not a permanent state. The Bible teaches at some point we will be awakened from our sleep and that's when we go to heaven. It could be a thousand years from the moment you die, but it will only feel like a moment.

People during this time didn't have the same fairytale version of heaven that we have today. They were okay with the unknown—with knowing that there was a God and that there was a heaven, but not needing the details all worked out.

All we can make is educated guesses here; and my guess is Lazarus probably saw nothing. That it was like waking from a coma—he was groggy, tired, and confused—but he had no memory of what happened while he was asleep.

Of course, this could all be wrong; it could be that we hop on the great elevator to heaven after we die, and if that's the case Lazarus probably did see something. But that's missing the point. Lazarus wasn't just a miracle—it was symbolic of what was to come: that all of us are in a dead-state and we need Christ to be raised—to be born again. Christ was showing people that everyone—Lazarus, Mary, you, me—that we all need him to be raised from the dead. The miracle isn't that he was raised from the physical dead—the miracle is that any one of us can be raised from the spiritual dead.

Scott Douglas

EPILOGUE

....

LAZARUS IS...

Most of us know Lazarus as that guy Jesus brought back from the dead. But different religions—notably Catholics, Orthodox and Muslims—have slightly different interpretations of who he is.

If you are sitting there thinking, wait! Did he just say Muslims? Yes! Lazarus is an important figure to the religion of Islam. He is not in the Quran, but he does show up a lot in Islamic artwork—especially during the medieval period.

Jesus is an important prophet to Muslims; they view him in a way that's similar to how

Christians see him—with the chief exception being they don't think he is the Messiah. While the Quran does not say that Jesus raised Lazarus, it does say that he raised the dead.

In the Catholic Church there are two saints named Lazarus; one is the Lazarus in Luke—the beggar; and one is Lazarus of Bethany. The beggar is the patron saint of lepers. According to Catholic tradition, Lazarus was beheaded and died in France.

Finally there's Orthodox Christians. Lazarus is so important to them that they gave him his very own holiday: Lazarus Saturday.

Lazarus Saturday happens the day before Palm Sunday (one week before Easter).

Lazarus isn't just that guy Jesus brought back from the dead—Lazarus is that guy he used to show us what it meant to be born again. What it meant to know that Jesus died so that we might live.

Lazarus of Bethany

···

APPENDIX: HOW TO BECOME A LAZARUS PILGRIM

Now that you've filled your mind with Lazarus, if you are ready to step it up and become a Lazarus pilgrim, these are all the must sights from around the world that you should see.

THE TOMB OF LAZARUS
(Al-Hardub Street, Al-Elzariya)

Obviously, the first spot on any pilgrim's list is the place where it all went down (supposedly). Lazarus' tomb is located in a cozy spot surrounded by not one, not two, but three churches! One a Muslim mosque, one Catholic, and one Orthodox. So I guess they really have something for everyone.

The actual location is obviously disputed, but you can tell by the public domain photo below that the pilgrims in the photo were pretty excited about it. You can also tell in the photo that the tomb isn't all that remarkable. Would it be cool to stand in the very place that Jesus' feet had touched? Sure! But cooler is to understand that Jesus' whole spiritual body is inside you and in reality, the tomb was probably in a different location, so the idea that you are stepping on the same dirt as Jesus is just an illusion—it's also an illusion that I thought the last sentence should not have been broken into two sentence, but I digress.

Loyal pilgrims are going to also want to visit not only where Lazarus was buried the first time, but where he was buried the second. And for that, as we've learned in this book, it gets a little more tricky. Several places hold this claim. So if you are a Lasso purest, you'll just have to visit all of them.[37]

CHURCH OF SAINT LAZARUS
(Πλατεία, Αγίου Λαζάρου, Λάρνακα)

---

[37] Make sure and send me a postcard.

No tour of the Mediterranean should be complete without a tour of this church in Cyprus. You'll have plenty to see while on the island because Barnabas, Paul, and John Mark also made visits to the island leaving many other things to see.

THE CATHEDRAL OF SAINT LAZARUS OF AUTUN
(Place du Terreau, 71400 Autun, France)

If you hold to the medieval theory that Lazarus made his way to France, then you'll have to make the voyage to Autun, France to see his second resting place.

VÉZELAY ABBEY
(89450 Vézelay, France)

If you happen to be on a Mary Magdalene pilgrimage, then pop on into the Vezelay Abbey, which is said to contain many of her relics; while you are there ask about Lazarus' tomb.

TRINITY ABBEY
(Hotel du Saillant, 47/49 Parc Ronsard, 41100 Vendôme, France)

And finally, what pilgrimage is complete without getting in at least one crazy relic? If you aren't familiar with the term, relics are basically objects that are associated with a particular saint or religious figure. Relics were an easy way for churches to make money centuries ago; if you could get your hands on an interesting relic, then suddenly you were on the map for tourism. People would visit your church from afar and leave generous offerings.

There are some real odd ones out there. How weird? Heads, fingernail clippings, blood, foreskin—I kid you not! Foreskin! And even Mary's breast milk! You can probably guess that the likelihood of most of these relics were fabrications, but that didn't matter—not when the money was pouring in.

For Lazarus, the crown jewel of relics is the tear Jesus shed when he learned of Lazarus' death. You read that right. This relic presupposes that someone saw Jesus cry and thought, "Hey! We need to go grab that tear and preserve it, so one day in the future people can go to a church in France to see it." It shouldn't be too surprising that the relic made its way here; it's only about 180 miles from the church in Autun, so Lazarus definitely made his mark on the region.

Scott Douglas

DISCUSSION QUESTIONS

INTRODUCTION

- Before reading any further, who is Lazarus to you?
- Why do you think Jesus raised Lazarus from the dead?
- Share what you think is the significance of the miracle.

CHAPTER ONE

- Have you ever personally (or known someone who has) had a near death experience—or been brought back from the dead?
- Why would some people be brought back from the dead and others not?
- Share a time when you prayed for something but it wasn't answered; was it ever answered?

- Share a time when you prayed for something and it was answered in an unexpected way.
- Do you think God answers all of your prayers?
- What can we learn from other people who were raised from the dead in both the Old and New Testaments?

CHAPTER TWO

- For you, how is John different than other Gospels?
- Why do you think there are four Gospels? Is it *really* important to have four different accounts of the same story?
- When you think about God, is your relationship more spiritual (you like to feel and dwell in God's presence)? Philosophical (God speaks to you in deeper thought—learning and reading, for example)? Or something else?
- Which of the seven miracles in John speaks to you most?

- Does "New Creation Theology" make you see John's Gospel in a different way?
- Where else in the Bible have you noticed literary devices being used to reveal God's truth?

CHAPTER THREE

- What do you think is the significance of Jesus waiting two days before going to Lazarus?
- The inclusion of women in the Gospel was somewhat radical; why did John include them?
- What does "Jesus wept" mean to you?
- Did you feel spiritually dead before accepting Christ? If you've never accepted Christ into your heart, do you feel like it's a necessary step to feel the presence of God in your life?
- Why aren't there more stories of the dead being raised?
- After Lazarus was raised from the dead, Jesus was essentially a marked man; it's fair to say if he would not have per-

formed this miracle, he might not have been persecuted. Why do you think he chose to go? Why did he go to the cross at all? Why couldn't he continue teaching and reveal the truth of God without dying for the sins of mankind—couldn't he have just forgiven without death?

EPILOGUE

- How do you see Lazarus after reading this book? Has your view changed at all?
- Why don't you think we heard a lot about Lazarus after he was brought back from the dead?
- If you've ever been to Jerusalem in person and saw the Tomb, share your story.

INDEX

Scott Douglas

ORGANIC FAITH SERIES

The *Organic Faith* series began as a question: how do we take away all the additives the church has added to Christianity over the past thousand years and return to the foundation of Christ's teachings?

Each book in the series looks at theology at its purest state and tries to reflect on ideas that are either forgotten or just not talked about.

The series takes sometimes complicated Biblical topics, and helps you reconsider them in ways you may have never thought about before.

The first book in the series is *Jesus Ascended. What Does That Mean?* It's available for purchase now wherever books are sold (digital, print and audio available).

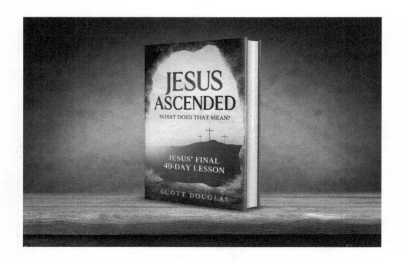

The next book, *Bethlehem, the Year Jesus Was Born* is a fresh take on Christmas. It strips away all the traditions we've attached to it and looks at it from the purest state. It's available for purchase now wherever books are sold (digital, print and audio available).

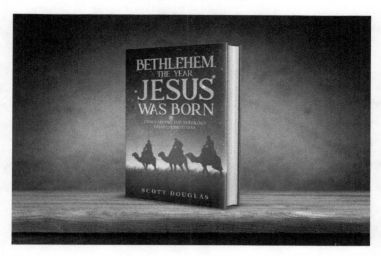

Related to the series, but not part of the series, is *Job Grieved*; it's a devotional of the Book of Job that I wrote after the death of my son. It's an encouraging read for anyone who is grieving the loss of someone in their life. It's available for purchase now wherever books are sold (digital and print available).

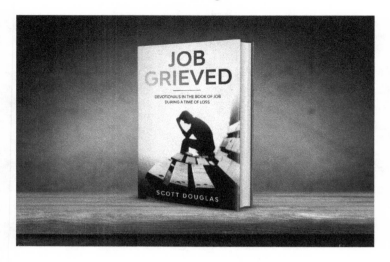

More books in the series are on the way! Make sure and sign up for the newsletter to find out more: https://www.jesusascended.com/newsletter

Lazarus of Bethany

ALSO BY SCOTT DOUGLAS

Bethlehem, the Year Jesus Was Born (2020) – Christian History

When you begin to unwrap the many layers of the first Christmas, you begin to see that there's more to Christmas than meets the eye. God is giving us a message—a gift to unwrap. This book helps us slow down and unpack the layers so we can see just how beautiful this gift really is.

Remedial Me (2020) – Humor / Essay Collection

Douglas explores his typical childhood......you know the kind where you have a grandpa that electrocutes you as a joke? Douglas also takes the reader on an epic quest to find prophylactics in Baton Rouge, how he failed the high school reading test, and much more! If you

need to find laugher in a world that sometimes feels void of it, then read on!

Jesus Ascended. What Does That Mean (2020) – Theology

Looking at what happened after the Resurrection, and further at the Ascension of Christ,
we start to see what happened to transform
the followers—and in seeing this we might
just be transformed ourselves. Something did
indeed happen during the forty days. Jesus
was not done teaching.

The Library Tree (2020) – Picture Book / Mythology

Do you know the real secret of libraries? For
hundreds of years, people have wrongly believed that books come from the minds of
writers. Librarians have kept the secret of
books' origins carefully guarded—but one day
a young reader named Tommy sees something
he wasn't supposed to: The Library Tree.

Job Grieved (2018) – Devotional / Grief

The Book of Job was radical in that it took out
the logic of loss—it said don't look for the logical argument for why bad things happen;
look to the healing.   If you are seeking the
"why" you will not find the answers in Job;
you will not find it anywhere in the Bible. But
if you want to heal your soul, then there's a
powerful message reading how Job deals with
grief.

#OrganicJesus (2016) – Apologetics

Consumers demand that their food be pesti-
cide-free, their cosmetics and shampoos be
paraben-free, and that everything possible—
from clothes to toilet paper—be made without
additives or chemicals. But there's nothing
that has more additives to the original product
than Christianity. How do we get back to the
100% organic version of Jesus?

The N00b Warriors Rebellion (2012) – YA

The war continues and a new, secret, front is emerging as a threat to both the Coco's and Frosted Flakes. As Dylan and Hunter learn more about the war, they are less eager to continue fighting—but the hope of finding their friend pushes them to continue.

The N00b Warriors (2010) – YA

Dylan Austin has grown up with the war as a constant background to his life; his dad has just returned from war missing a leg; his older sister is missing and presumed dead from the war; and all through school war has been embedded into everything they teach. Teens have been raised on educational war video games, and their minds are polluted with the idea that war is just a game.

Quiet, Please: Dispatches from a Public Librarian (2008) – Humor / Memoir

Note: this book was originally released by Da Capo book; it was reissued independently when the rights reverted back to me.

For most of us, librarians are the quiet people behind the desk, who, apart from the occasional "shush," vanish into the background. But in Quiet, Please, McSweeney's contributor Scott Douglas puts the quirky caretakers of our literature front and center. With a keen eye for the absurd and a Kesey-esque cast of characters (witness the librarian who is sure Thomas Pynchon is Julia Roberts's latest flame), Douglas takes us where few readers have gone before.   Punctuated by his own highly subjective research into library history—from Andrew Carnegie's Gilded Age to today's Afghanistan—Douglas gives us a surprising (and sometimes hilarious) look at the lives which make up the social institution that is his library.

Lazarus of Bethany

MORE TO COME

Many years ago, I wrote humor for the now defunct Christian humor magazine the *Wittenburg Door*. If you'd like to read the parodies I wrote there, join my newsletter list and I'll send you out a free copy.

Join here: https://www.jesusascended.com/newsletter

In addition to a free book, I'll occasionally (interpret as hardly ever) email you about new books and other writing news you might enjoy.

Lazarus of Bethany

Scott Douglas

ABOUT THE AUTHOR

Scott Douglas wrote this about page, which, he admits, makes him sound a bit like a narcissist; so narcissistically speaking, Douglas is the esteemed author of a memoir about his experience working in a public library (*Quiet,*

Please: Dispatches from a Public Librarian), an ongoing YA series (*The N00b Warriors*), and two technical books on iPhone app development (*Going Mobile* and *Build Your Own Apps for Fun and Profit*). Esteemed writing aside, Douglas teaches humor and memoir writing for the Gotham Writers Workshops. He lives in Anaheim, but to sound cooler, he usually says he "lives five minutes from Disneyland." He lives with his wife, Diana, in a home that is a registered California landmark.

If you enjoyed this book, you may also enjoy his apologetics work *#OrganicJesus: Finding Your Way to an Unprocessed, GMO-Free Christianity* (Kregel 2016)

If Scott Douglas did not write this about page, it would read:

> Scott Douglas lives in Anaheim with his wife. He is the author of other books. He likes to think that his organic deodorant holds back his BO for more

than 30 minutes, but who is he kidding?

You can connect with him here: http://www.scottdouglas.org/contact.html

Lazarus of Bethany

Scott Douglas

EXCERPT FROM "JESUS ASCENDED: WHAT DOES THAT MEAN?"

Scott Douglas

INTRODUCTION

···

S O M E T H I N G   H A P P E N E D

Something happened.

Jesus rose. We hear about it every Easter. We sing songs about it. We even have an Easter Bunny to symbolize the event.[38]

But Christ didn't just rise from the dead. He ascended to Heaven.

We hear the stories about Peter and John and all the heroes of the New Testament, and they're unstoppable Christians—fearless and bold. And sometimes we wrongly assume that they just got that way. That Christ died for their sins, and bam! They're instantly changed! On the contrary, the disciples were actually quite cowardly in their actions after the Resurrection.

---

[38] Fun fact about Easter Bunnies—people used to believe that they were hermaphrodites (i.e., they could reproduce without having sex). You know who else could do that? The Virgin Mary! Hence, the Easter Bunny was born.

It wasn't until after the Ascension that they were on fire for Christ. So, what happened during the forty days? Something happened.

You'd think that everyone and their brother would want to talk about an event that incredible. But you'd be wrong. And it leaves us with more than a few questions.

Where do you go if you want to understand what happened? Matthew? You won't find it there. Mark? Kind of, but it's text that most Bible scholars now accept was not in the earliest version. What about John? Surely good old John would have a lot to say! Not exactly. He talks about Jesus doing miracles, but nowhere in John does he ascend to Heaven.

So how is it that Christians came to believe that Jesus not only rose from the dead, but stuck around forty days before ascending to Heaven? That's where Luke comes in. Luke is the only Gospel that talks at any length (even though it's short passages) about Jesus ascending. He does so in both the Gospel of Luke and the Acts of the Apostles, which he also authored.

Sprinkled throughout the Bible are references to the Ascension, which tells us that it was something early Christians believed. The Apostle Peter believed it,[39] as did the Apostle

---

[39] 1 Peter 3:13-22

Paul,[40] and it's fair to say that all the other apostles did as well.[41]

So important is the doctrine, that the original statement of belief that most Christians (Catholic, Protestant, and Orthodox) go to—the Nicene Creed—includes it. That means if you belong to any of those groups, you are kind of supposed to believe in the Ascension.[42]

#   #   #

A Not Completely Necessary Detour of Empty Tomb Theories

The point of this book isn't to prove that the Resurrection is real; there are plenty of books on that. Still, as a reference only, I will note the popular theories about what else could have happened.

The LCD Theory

This theory says what is depicted in the Bible is really just a series of hallucinations. That makes sense. It might even be logical. But there are two problems:

First, more than one person saw him—even 500 at one time. If Peter saw him but no one else did, it would be

---

[40] Ephesians 4:8-10

[41] See Appendix A for a more complete list of Ascension references.

[42] Even if you don't have the slightest idea about what it is or means.

So, what's the deal with the Ascension anyway? Shouldn't this be plastered all over the place? Wouldn't there have been a giant atomic bomb-sized glorious viewing that you could see all the way from Rome? Why did only believers see it?

First, it is referenced outside the Bible—more on that in later chapters.

Second, we have to consider the nature of Christ. He performed miracles, but that was never his ministry. He didn't come to Earth to be the flashy miracle guy. His ministry was the way he lived his life.

People frequently say, "If there is a God, then why doesn't he announce it?" What I often think about this phrase is "Doesn't he?" Every day, things happen that are beyond science—things that can only be described by the word miraculous. They deeply move us—heck sometimes we even like them on Facebook. But the thing is, miracles are forgotten pretty quickly. You are quicker to forget a miracle than you are a simple kind gesture in a time of need.

And let's not forget, if God did announce himself, the whole freewill thing would go out the window. If we could walk outside right now, look up and see God up in the sky, then why wouldn't we believe in him? But unfortunately, on Earth we can't have that kind of relationship.

So, in answer to that question about why people didn't see it from miles away, the reason is probably as simple as it was not all that spectacular. Jesus didn't ride up to Heaven on an atomic bomb with a cowboy hat, shooting out fire-works from his eyeballs. It was more likely a beautifully intimate moment witnessed by those closest to him. It wasn't meant for the entire Roman Empire to see.

#   #   #

So, we have this intimate event that only a select few even saw. Great. But why is that event even important?

Close your eyes and take a road trip through history with me; we're about to get Biblical, so buckle in.[43]

Think back to those early Sunday school stories; the ones about the fall of Eden, Noah, the Tower of Babel, Moses. They're great stories and even better lessons for history… but they also have a theme. The entire Old Testament has a theme, in fact. God's people mess up and they fall; God picks them up and they excel; God's people mess up and they fall; God picks them up and they excel. It's like a bad broken record. If you've ever read the Old Testament from cover to cover, you probably asked yourself at least fifty times, "Seriously, what's wrong with these people? Why can't they just listen to God?!"

The Jewish people were privileged in the sense that they knew no matter how badly they screwed up, God would eventually rescue them, and all would be well again. They expected it. The prophets predicting a Messiah who would rule over them should really not be all that surprising—of

---

[43] Don't worry, we'll stick to Sunday school stories.

course God would send someone to rescue them. They had messed up, and the kingdom God had given them with David had been taken away, so of course a new king from David's line would come and rescue them. That's just the way God did things—God's redemption was just as predictable as Israel's sin.

The Ascension is the fulfillment of this promise. When Jesus left Earth, he created a new kingdom in the line of David in Heaven. This pattern of God's people sinning, and God's people being redeemed could finally be resolved once and for all.

Lots of men and women have been raised from the dead; the Resurrection of Christ is really nothing special. Sure, it's an amazing, unexplained feat that can only be attributed to divine intervention, but pause for a moment and ask: what's so special about the Resurrection? Christ raised dead people; so did his disciples. Yeah, it's pretty amazing that he rose from the dead, but if that in itself is enough to worship a person, shouldn't we also be praying to people like Lazarus?[44]

The amazing thing about the Resurrection is not the act, but the act that followed—the theology that feels more like a footnote in history: The Ascension. Which leaves us with a very important question to ask: If it's so important, then why is it only mentioned in the Gospel of Luke? Why isn't the Ascension mentioned more often in the Gospels?

---

[44] Lazarus, for those who need a reminder, came back to life after being dead for four days after Jesus came and woke him up.

First, let's consider dates. More than likely, Luke and John were the last Gospels written, which means they had more time to digest things. The Resurrection, by human standards, is more fascinating to tell, and there's a chance that the early writers of the Gospel hadn't quite considered the significance of what happened.

Let's also considered the missing fragment of Mark; it cuts off in a very unusual place. Most scholars agree that the ending in place was not by the original author...but most scholars also believe where it cuts off isn't the original ending. So, what are we left with? The most popular theory is that while the added text isn't completely Mark, it isn't completely not Mark either. What does that mean? It means there's a very strong chance that the original version of Mark did mention the Ascension—just not quite like the translator wrote it—perhaps with different syntax, but the same meaning.

The most important thing to remember about the Gospels is they were written with an audience in mind. Think about Abraham Lincoln; there have been over 15,000 books written about him. How can people still make money writing about Lincoln? Easy...they write about him from different angles that people haven't considered. Some biographers will spend little or no time writing about Lincoln's death because that's not what their book is about. So, when we think about why the Gospels each wrote different accounts of the post-Resurrection, it's because each one was writing for a different purpose.

\#   \#   \#

The Audience of the Gospels

There's a lot to digest, so let's take a short break. As we consider why the Ascension isn't clearly recorded in all the Gospels, let's consider the purpose of each Gospel (i.e. who they were writing to and what their intent was).

Matthew

Audience: Early tradition said the Gospel of Matthew was written by Matthew, the disciple; more recent scholars tend to believe that because Matthew seems to use Mark as a source, it may have been someone else. Whatever the case, the Gospel of Matthew seems to have been written with Jews in mind; Matthew wanted to prove that Christ was the Messiah that the Jewish people had been waiting for.

Resurrection Message: The Gospel of Matthew ends with the Great Commission, in which Jesus instructs the disciples to go and make disciples of all nations. It's fitting that Matthew ended with Jesus telling the disciples to go and convert, because that's what his Gospel was all about—to tell the good news and teach about the new covenant.

Mark

Audience: Like Matthew, it's difficult to say who the author of Mark's Gospel is, but it's traditionally held that the

The Resurrection was great. I believe in it. I believe it was miraculous. But I don't believe that Christ is Lord because he rose from the dead.

There's more written about Christ's ministry before his death than the events that happened after his Resurrection, but when we look at Ascension, we begin to see that there's power in small details. We begin to see that something happened after the Resurrection—something happened to transform the lives of believers and make them more than followers.

The problem with the Resurrection of Christ is as believers we have a tendency to believe in the miracle and not the theology. When we look at what happened after the Resurrection, and further at the Ascension of Christ, we begin to see what happened to transform the followers—and in seeing this we might just be transformed ourselves.

Something did indeed happen during the forty days; why didn't God spend more time revealing? That's something that we will not know on Earth. But when we look at what he does reveal in the Ascension, we begin to see that Jesus was not done teaching; and as we begin to understand these teachings, we will be transformed ourselves.

UNSTOPPABLE CHRISTIANS

Scott Douglas

Lazarus of Bethany

ONE

....

JESUS APPEARS TO THE MARYS

More people believe in angels than in hell. And why not? It's far easier to believe in good things than bad. Unfortunately, most people believe in the Nicolas Cage kind of angels;[45] the kind of angel that humans can actually become if they're swell people; the kind that have wings and float around just waiting to save us. That's not necessarily false, but it's not exactly Biblical.[46]

So, when the gospels record angels at the empty tomb of Christ, it's important to remember what angels are in the Bible—to put it simply, angels are messengers from God.

There's an important lesson to be learned about the women Jesus is about to appear to, but before we get to that, we have to understand the angels.

---

[45] Fun fact—City of Angels steals several plot points from Hans Christian Andersen's *The Little Mermaid*.

[46] Meg Ryan isn't even a Bible name.

Depending on the gospel account, there was between one to four angels at the tomb; contradictory, right? Not exactly. Remember, the Gospels are four different writers with four different purposes writing for four different audiences. They aren't contradicting each other; they're recording different aspects of the same story.

The greater importance isn't on the detail—how many angels there were—it's on the meaning of the details. What, if anything, do the angels mean? If angels are Heavenly messengers, then what is it that they are announcing?

First, it's obvious that their message is that Jesus has resurrected, and he is the Messiah. Just as gospels noted that angels were there to announce his birth, they are there to announce his resurrection.

But there's more. The Gospel of John gives an important detail in 20:11. He says that two angels were sitting.

Impressive, right? It's not every day you read about two angels sitting on the job. More curious, however, is not what they're doing, but where they're doing it—they're sitting where Jesus' body was only a short time ago.

It's time to get all Old Testament. The Old Testament is notorious for laws—lots and lots of laws.[47] Some laws that

---

[47] 613 laws to be exact.

make sense[48] and some are a little...odd.[49] But tucked in there with all of those laws is a lot of stuff about a certain Ark of the Covenant. The Ark was built in Moses' time and they took that bad boy everywhere. It represented God's covenant with the Israelites and it's a permanent fixture throughout the Old Testament.

So, what does that have to do with two angels sitting where Jesus was? On top of the Ark were statues of two cherubim—or angels.

What the Gospel of John is painting is a real-life Ark of the Covenant. They aren't just sitting back on the tomb's recliners—they're sitting on the stone that held Jesus' body; John's record is saying, "Guess what? There's a new covenant in town."

#   #   #

When Apple rolls out a new iPhone, what do they do? They hold a big press conference that's meant to get their base followers excited and then they'll go out and tell their friends who will also get excited, and before you know it millions of people have new phones. Every company uses the same strategy—market to your base—your product evangelist.

---

[48] There's one God; worship him.

[49] They made sense thousands of years ago, but they really have no importance today.

It makes sense that God would market his new covenant the same way—he'd tell his disciples all about it, so they could go spread the news to the world. But something un-usual happens on the way to the podium to make the big an-nouncement—God markets it to the audience you'd least likely suspect: the women.

It would be like Apple going to a third world where there's absolute zero cellular signal, Wi-Fi, or electricity and saying, "Isn't this cool?" I'm sure they'd think it was pretty amazing, but what are they supposed to do with it?

Today a woman is just as likely to start a revolution as a man; two thousand years ago? Not so much. So, what is God thinking? What's he trying to teach us here?

If you are a Bible conspiracy theorist, then it isn't at all surprising—Jesus was, after all, doing the old bait n' tackle with her; hints and blatant descriptions of Jesus and Mary locking lips are in all the ancient manuscripts. Unfortunately for Biblical conspiracy theorists, the ancient manuscripts come to light too long after Jesus' life to make them any-thing but just stories people were telling. The simple fact is there's nothing in the Gospels to suggest that Jesus was in-volved in a relationship with Mary.[50]

So, if it's not because he wanted to see his old sweet-heart, then why? Was it because he was a card-carrying member of the local feminist movement of Jerusalem, and

---

[50] In the words of Seinfeld, "Not that there's anything wrong with that"—it just didn't happen.

he wanted to set his boys straight on who he *really* loves? Not likely.[51]

So, what gives? There are 11 confused men who risk an awful lot to follow Jesus. Couldn't Jesus have done them a solid and let them know all was well? Of course! But he didn't…and that certainly begs the question why.

On the surface, the best reason is simply because the Marys were the least likely suspects for a crime. If one of the disciples had gotten to the tomb first, then people could have more easily said they stole his body—heck, they didn't even go to the tomb first and people still say this!

The fact that it was a woman who was the first eyewitness makes it more believable for the mere fact that women would not be able to carry out the plot to steal his body—they'd have to roll away a large stone, carry a rather heavy body, and fight off Roman guards. There are plenty of women who could carry off this plot—they're called women warriors and they're champions in swordplay; Brienne of Tarth from *Game of Thrones*—she might be able to pull it off…but these women? Not so much.

But God rarely teaches us things on the surface. There's something much deeper and personal about what's about to happen. The disciples had a much different relationship with Jesus than the women did.

---

[51] Jesus was pretty radical in thinking with regard to women, but his appearance here doesn't seem to imply it has anything to do with making a feminist statement.

The first lesson Jesus gives post-Resurrection is about the relationship we can have with him.

#   #   #

Before getting too far along, let's address the elephant in the room. The women appear first in all four of the Gospels…kind of. When you read all the accounts side by side,[52] each gospel tells a slightly different story. Some mention that Jesus appeared in front of several women, others say it was only Mary Magdalene. Some say Mary went to the tomb, saw it was empty, told the others, then went back to the tomb.

So, are we really to believe that the Gospel is to be trusted when we have four different books saying four contradictory things? If they got this all messed up, they must have gotten the rest all messed up. That's certainly a fair point, but to call the accounts contradictory is a bit extreme—and wrong.

In reality, it can be assumed it was several women, but because Mary Magdalene was kind of like the Peter of women, that's who they mentioned.[53] As noted in the previous chapter, each author had a different audience; some of those audiences would have not known who all the Marys or other women were, but they definitely knew who Mary Magdalene was. It would be like a newspaper saying Pope

---

[52] For added challenge, you can also read them all upside-down.

[53] She's kind of a rock star.

Francis and Federico Lombardi flew to Germany to visit a church; Federico Lombardi is an important person in the Catholic Church, but most people don't know who he is—so what you are more likely to read is that Pope Francis flew to Germany to visit a church.

The different accounts are not an example of contradiction; rather, they are an example of different authors.

#   #   #

There's Something About Marys

Who were these women that all the Gospels mention? Let's pause for a section and get a pop-up mini biography.

MARY MAGDALENE

Luke 8:2 and Mark 16:9 say that she was a woman Jesus had cured and cast out seven demons from. Most see her as the person that women turned to as a leader in the early church—in the same way men might have looked at Peter. Some have called her a repentant prostitute, but this largely stems from the misunderstanding that she was the unnamed sinner who anoints Jesus' feet; most scholars agree that she was not. This misconception was helped along by Pope Gregory, who delivered a sermon that misattributed Mary with the unnamed sinner. Pope Gregory based this on the fact that the seven demons were really seven sins and those seven sins obviously represented her loose lifestyle. Speculation that she was in a relationship with Jesus was first seen in the Gospel of Philip; in it, Jesus is seen

The angels just performed the opening act of the most epic rock concert ever—now it's time for the main act to perform his final set list of teachings before ascending to Heaven—and spoiler alert, his set list includes all of his greatest hits. In John 20:16, Jesus starts with a bang when he says something incredibly telling. He says, "Mary."

At first glance, it doesn't seem like much, but let's look at what's going on.

Mary is an emotional wreck. Her savior is gone. She can't make sense of what's happened. She's a mess!

Jesus appears to her and she's so emotional that she doesn't even know who she's talking to. She's in complete denial.

It's in this denial that it gets interesting.

Mary just devoted years of her life devoted to following this guy and now he's alive and in the flesh standing right in front of her…and she has no clue that it's him! That's a little odd, isn't it? When odd things happen in the Bible, we should never just shrug and say, "That was weird" and move on. We should look at it curiously and say is there something more going on here?

There's definitely more going on here. The scene is a mirror image of us.

When we don't believe, we're in denial. Jesus is standing right in front of us, but we just think we're talking to a stranger and we don't recognize him. We can't see Jesus until we are ready to accept Jesus. And in that moment, Mary just isn't ready because she still can't comprehend any of it.

But with one word, Mary snaps out of it. She can see Jesus and it all makes sense. She knows who he is.

Jesus doesn't do what some of us might. If I'd just risen from the dead and appeared in front of my wife and she didn't know me, I wouldn't say, "Diana." I'd shake her and say, "Are you kidding me! All these years together and you don't know who I am? What the heck is wrong with you?" And then I'd storm off and pout.

But Jesus says, "Mary." And with that word she knows Jesus is alive and standing in front of her.

Jesus could have said any word, but he chose her name. To snap her out of her denial, he told her he knew her name—he knew who she was. It's an intimate gesture and what it shows is that Jesus knows each of us personally. He knows our name.

But here's the funny thing about what happens next. Mary and Jesus just had a moment. It's intimate. It's personal. It's time to hug it up. But that doesn't happen.

The touchy-feely Jesus that's all over the New Testament is suddenly a little less...touchy.

There are a lot of polar opposites in the post-Resurrection—things you'd expect to be happening aren't happening.

Mary goes for the hug and Jesus hug blocks her. John 20:17 says that Jesus told her not to touch him because he had not ascended to Heaven.

So, let's get this straight. Jesus—the guy Christians grow up believing we can have a personal relationship with is telling her she can't hug him? That doesn't seem too personal.

At face value, it's not personal at all. Later, Thomas gets to touch Jesus, so why him and not Mary?

The fact that Thomas could touch him but not Mary tells us that when Jesus says not to touch him, it's not because he can't be touched.

Mary wants to embrace him because she thinks it's back to the good old days—chilling in the countryside listening to amazing sermons, feeding thousands, and getting tipsy on the best water-to-wine ever made. But Jesus is telling her that the good old days are gone—she needs to know him differently now. The good old days are really in front of her, but she needs to come to understand what that means.

From that point on, he needed Mary to know that the relationship would be a spiritual one—not a physical one.

There are two Jesuses. Some of us only get to know one. There's the one we all come to know—the one who did amazing things. One might call him the historical Jesus. And then there's one we know if we commit our life to him; this is the spiritual Jesus.

Jesus' refusal to Mary isn't because she can't touch him; it's because she can't touch him like before.

Everyone wants to see Jesus. If they could just have a bit of proof, they'd believe. But that Jesus isn't here anymore. The Jesus we can know is the one we know spiritually.

But the one we know spiritually we can know much more intimately than the one who came in the flesh. Before the Resurrection, Jesus was the great teacher; what's happening is the start of the transformation for believers—they are about to go from students to teachers.

And finally, we come to what may be the most jarring verse of all to some readers—especially modern readers who are not reading the original translation and may miss the context. Jesus gives specific instructions to Mary; he says to tell them, "I am ascending to my Father and your Father, to my God and your God." (NIV) [54]

Huh?

First, let's consider something very important here. Jesus could have just as easily said "our Father" and "our God." He didn't.

Let's hit the rewind button here a second and visit just a few chapters prior: John 5:16-18.

---

[54] John 20:17

This is one of the first things that gets Jesus in a whirlwind of trouble with Jewish leaders. First, he heals on the Sabbath—a major no-no.[55] Jesus was a good talker; he probably could have gotten away with it by talking his way out, but he has no intention of running away. Instead he uses the phrase "My Father." That does it! The Jewish leaders are fuming because this phrase puts Jesus as an equal to God.

What Jesus is telling Mary is that he is equal to God… but he doesn't stop there. He is saying that the man upstairs is now "your Father" and "your God." Father is a reference to the divine nature of Christ, and God is a reference to his human nature (i.e., God in the Flesh). Christ has now secured our place and through him we can have unity with God.

Some of the Gospels simply reported that Mary and the others saw Jesus and he told them to go tell the disciples; that's essentially what John says. But John found it to be important to his message to relate what Jesus said to Mary.

John was traditionally the last Gospel written; perhaps in his old age, he had come to realize the importance women had played in Jesus' ministry and he wanted to portray them fairly. But more importantly, John wants his readers to know that they can have unity with God—that God doesn't have to be the mighty killjoy in the sky—that through Christ, we can have a relationship with God that's like belonging to a family.

---

[55] Sabbaths are for obeying God, not experiencing God.

There's going to be many lessons to transform the disciples lives post-Resurrection, but the first is about the relationship they now have with God.

Everyone knows the phrase, "You can have a personal relationship with God." But the nature of people can make that phrase carry less meaning, because Christians sometimes look at other Christians and expect them to have the same personal relationship that they have.

Having a personal relationship isn't about the other person. It's about you. Jesus Christ knows your name. He knows your struggles. Your pains. He knows your background. He knows what makes you angry; what makes you sad; what makes you want to give up—and what makes you want to keep going. He knows everything about you.

We all have struggles. Some of us it is addictions. Some of us it is pride. Some it is greed. Whatever it is: Jesus knows our name. He knows all of our weaknesses and he's returned to dwell inside us—to experience an intimacy with him that we would not know without the Resurrection.

But first we have to be like Mary: we have to see him. We can say we know Jesus just like Mary said she knew him. But knowing Jesus and seeing Jesus are two different things. We can go to church and know about Jesus—about his teachings, about what he did, and his theology; we can do all of that without ever really seeing Jesus—without ever really knowing what it means to have a true relationship with Jesus.

To see Jesus is to put all your pains aside and accept that Jesus really does want to dwell in you—he really does love you and he really is there with you. He really does know your name.

UNSTOPPABLE CHRISTIANS

Catherine of Siena is one of the top religious women of all time—right up there with Mary, Mary, and Other Mary. When most women of her day (she lived from 1347-1380) were content being submissive, she was quite the bad girl by actually using her mind and writing some of the greatest works of early Christian literature. Unfortunately, Catherine was also kind of anorexic for Jesus. Communion became one of her few meals in later life (and by later, we're talking late 20s).

Her fasting was legendary and ultimately fatal; by the age of 33, she could no longer eat or swallow water, and she died of a stroke. People of her day loved her—so much so that they wanted her body in Siena. But there was a problem—you couldn't just drag a smelly corpse out of Rome. Mourners decided that if they couldn't have the body, they could at least have the head. They chopped it off, stuffed it in a bag, and left for Siena; according to legends, when guards questioned what the foul-smelling bag was, they opened it up and there were roses inside. Fans of the morbid can see the head for themselves by visiting the Basilica di San Domenico.

Scott Douglas

End of Excerpt

Jesus Ascended. What Does That Mean? Is available in print, digital, and audio wherever books are sold. Your support is appreciated, but anyone without means to purchase the book can reach out to the author for a copy.

Scott Douglas